1

Table of Contents

> *"[W]hen any of our citizens are unable to fulfill their potential due to factors that have nothing to do with their talent, character, or work ethic, then I believe that there's a role for our government to play."*
>
> *—President Obama at the signing of Executive Order 13515: Participation of Asian Americans and Pacific Islanders in Federal Programs, October 14, 2009*

Since the signing of Executive Order 13515, the White House Initiative on Asian Americans and Pacific Islanders (Initiative) engaged 23 Federal departments and agencies to focus on the unmet needs of Asian Americans and Pacific Islanders (AAPIs). Each of the Federal agencies began reviewing and assessing their programs and services in August 2010, compiling data relevant to AAPIs and soliciting input from the AAPI community and the President's Advisory Commission on AAPIs. The cross-departmental efforts were coordinated through an Interagency Working Group, co-chaired by Commerce Secretary Gary Locke and Education Secretary Arne Duncan, and coordinated by Initiative Executive Director Kiran Ahuja and members of the Interagency Implementation Team (IIT).

These efforts culminated in Agency Plans designed to meet the needs of the AAPI community while leveraging the dynamic community assets that work to meet those needs. The Plans address the Initiative's cross-cutting priorities: improving data collection, analysis and dissemination of AAPI-specific information; ensuring linguistic and culturally competent access to Federal programs and services; protecting civil rights and equal opportunity; promoting and increasing Federal employment among AAPIs; and increasing outreach and access to Federal grant opportunities and other programs.

> *"Each executive department and agency designated by the Initiative shall prepare a plan (agency plan) for, and shall document, its efforts to improve the quality of life of Asian Americans and Pacific Islanders through increased participation in Federal programs in which Asian Americans and Pacific Islanders may be underserved."*
>
> *—Executive Order 13515: Increasing Participation of Asian Americans and Pacific Islanders in Federal Programs, signed by President Obama, October 14, 2009*

Agency Plan Snapshot of Cross-cutting Goals

Data: Ten agencies commit to improving the collection, analysis and dissemination of data on AAPI communities.

Language Access: Twenty agencies address linguistically and culturally competent access to their Federal programs and services.

Civil Rights: Thirteen agencies seek to protect civil rights and equal opportunity for AAPIs specifically.

Federal Employment: Fifteen agencies actively promote and seek to increase Federal employment among AAPIs.

Outreach: Nineteen agencies increase outreach and access to Federal grant programs for the AAPI community.

In addition, the Agency Plans tackle the Initiative's issue-specific priority areas: Healthy Communities, Sustainable Neighborhoods, Educational Opportunities, Economic Growth and Civil Rights. Working closely with members of the IIT, the Initiative aligns its cross-cutting and issue-specific goals with those in the Agency Plans to ensure coordinated implementation.

In the State of the Union, President Obama spoke of the need to maintain America's leadership in a rapidly changing world so that our economy is competitive, growing, and working for all Americans. To do so, he put forward a plan to help the United States win the future by out-innovating, out-educating and out-building our global competitors. The Initiative Agency Plans help achieve the Administration's goals by investing in the AAPI community in the following ways:

Innovate

The U.S. Department of Health and Human Services is developing innovative programs to improve the health and wellness of NHPIs through the Community Health Data Initiative and by providing funding to programs that address NHPI health and well-being and encouraging research projects that target diseases and conditions that disproportionately impact NHPI communities.

The U.S. Department of Agriculture is integrating culturally relevant foods in nutrition information provided by the Food and Nutrition Service, the Center for Nutrition Policy and Promotion and the National Institute of Food Agriculture.

The U.S. Environmental Protection Agency is coordinating an intra-agency Nail Care Project among its regional offices and developing Train-the-Trainers workshops for nail salon workers to educate them about environmental workplace hazards.

Educate

The U.S. Department of Education is improving access and increasing technical assistance and outreach to institutions that qualify for the Asian American and Native American Pacific Islander Serving Institutions (AANAPISI) program in order to increase the number of AAPI students who finish college.

The National Aeronautics and Space Administration is promoting the availability of NASA content to AAPI educators and offering distance learning programs through the NASA Digital Learning Network.™

The U.S. Department of Veterans Affairs is partnering with Asian American and Native American Pacific Islander Serving Institutions and AAPI national and community groups to promote and support summer internship programs.

Build

The Federal Communications Commission is improving AAPI digital literacy by providing translations of consumer-oriented broadband materials into numerous Asian languages including Japanese, Hmong and Cambodian.

The U.S. Department of Commerce is planning to increase the number of small and medium AAPI businesses that export to an additional country by providing export-related training and business-to-business networking sessions to minority-owned companies.

The U.S. Equal Employment Opportunity Commission is partnering with the U.S. Office of Personnel Management to create and implement a pilot program to begin collecting AAPI workforce and complaint race and national origin data at three Federal agencies.

The Initiative will further develop its relationships with the agencies over the next year to implement their ambitious agendas and continue its work to improve the quality of life and opportunities for AAPIs through increased access to, and participation in, Federal programs and services.

This document contains summaries of the Agency Plans. To view the full set of plans, please visit http://www.aapi.gov and follow the "Agency Implementation Plans" link.

Mission. The U.S. Department of Agriculture (USDA) provides federal leadership on food, agriculture, natural resources, rural development, nutrition, and related issues based on sound public policy, the best available science, and efficient management. USDA strives to expand economic opportunity through innovation, helping rural America to thrive; to promote agriculture production sustainability that better nourishes Americans while also helping feed others throughout the world; and to preserve and conserve our Nation's natural resources through restored forests, improved watersheds, and healthy private working lands.

PRIORITY PROGRAM GOALS FOR THE ASIAN AMERICAN AND PACIFIC ISLANDER COMMUNITY

Per Executive Order 13515, USDA has identified four high-priority goals that will span the next two years. These goals will help increase the AAPI community's participation in and access to the agency's programs.

Goal 1. ***Improve health outcomes for AAPIs through their expanded access to USDA information about nutrition, physical activity, and food safety, and their increased participation in USDA nutrition assistance programs.***
Activities include integrating food nutrition information on ten culturally relevant foods into USDA nutrition materials; translating food safety materials into AAPI languages; increasing AAPI participation in community extension programs about nutrition, food safety and related topics; implementing a targeted outreach program in 5 areas of the US with high pockets of food-insecure AAPIs focused on improving their access to USDA feeding programs; and collaborating with federal, state, local and NGO partners to increase involvement of AAPI adults and children in nutrition/physical activity programs, particularly for children at the K-12 levels.

Goal 2. ***Strengthen environmental quality and sustainable environmental practices in communities with AAPI farmers and ranchers.***
Activities include targeted outreach to increase participation by eligible AAPI farmers and ranchers in USDA programs to improve on- and off-farm environmental quality, under auspices of USDA's Natural Resource Conservation Service, Farm Service Agency, and Forest Service.

Goal 3. ***Improve understanding of the economic needs of AAPIs in rural America and increase their participation in USDA programs focused on rural development, farm economics and risk management.***
Activities include developing focused studies on rates of participation by AAPIs in USDA programs; improving USDA employees' understanding of AAPI cultural needs and specialty/niche crops; and implementing a new rural outreach campaign highlighting the Rural Micro-Entrepreneurs Assistance Program, and value-added resources for improving farm economics, including niche crops.

Goal 4. ***Ensure that AAPIs have equal access to USDA programs and services, and employment opportunities.***
Activities include focused analysis of civil rights program complaints; identification of best program practices; strengthened AAPI access to translated materials for USDA programs, projects, and initiatives; increased recruitment efforts to attract greater numbers of AAPI applicants for federal positions.

Mission. The U.S. Department of Commerce (Commerce) advances economic growth, jobs and opportunities for the American people. It has cross cutting responsibilities in the areas of trade, technology, entrepreneurship, economic development, environmental stewardship and statistical research and analysis.

The products and services the Department provides touch the lives of Americans and American companies in many ways, including weather forecasts, the decennial census, and patent and trademark protection for inventors and businesses.

The development of commerce to provide new opportunities was the central goal at the department's beginning in 1903 and it remains a primary obligation today.

PRIORITY PROGRAM GOALS FOR THE ASIAN AMERICAN AND PACIFIC ISLANDER COMMUNITY

Per Executive Order 13515, Commerce has identified three high-priority goals that will span across the next two years. These goals will help increase the AAPI community's participation in and access to the agency's programs.

Goal 1. ***Increase the annual number of Small and Medium-size Enterprises (SMEs) the Commercial Service assists in exporting to an additional country by 40 percent.***
In President Obama's State of the Union Address on January 27, 2010, he announced the National Export Initiative, a critical new effort that will lead to long-term, sustainable economic growth for the United States. The President has a goal of doubling exports over the next five years, an increase that will support two million American jobs.

Commerce is committed to helping businesses including AAPI-owned businesses to grow through global trade. To help minority-owned businesses globalize their business models, the Minority Business Development Agency (MBDA) has developed a strategic partnership with the International Trade Administration, to provide export related training to minority-owned companies.

In addition, MBDA will be providing business-to-business networking sessions to link minority-owned companies to global opportunities. MBDA is building relationships with OPIC, EX-IM Bank and various other government agencies that can provide financial support for the companies.

Goal 2. ***Increase the AAPI community's access to federal funding.***
Commerce administers a number of grant programs. These grants range from grants that help foster economic development and competitiveness in a region to providing funds to entities that are equipped to provide technical assistance for minority businesses. Commerce is committed to developing an outreach strategy that ensures the AAPI community will have access to these grant programs.

Goal 3. ***Foster the recruitment, career development and advancement of AAPIs in the Federal Government.***
Commerce understands the importance of diversity in the workforce and professional development in the workplace. Commerce is committed to developing a plan which includes working closely with Asian American and Native American Pacific Islander Serving Institutions and increasing leadership activities that highlight diversity.

Mission. The U.S. Department of Defense (DoD) provides the military forces needed to deter war and to protect the security of our country.

PRIORITY PROGRAM GOALS FOR THE ASIAN AMERICAN AND PACIFIC ISLANDER COMMUNITY

Per Executive Order 13515, DoD has identified three high-priority goals that will span the next two years. These goals will help increase the AAPI community's participation in and access to the agency's programs.

Goal 1. ***Strengthen and improve support for AAPI Wounded Warriors, Transitioning Service Members, and their Families and Caregivers.***

Our generation of AAPI heroes faces many challenges when they return home. Many are recovering from wounds (both visible and invisible) and others face the daunting task of finding a job in today's economy. The DoD is focused on the care for our wounded warriors, transitioning service members, and their families and caregivers. There are many programs and resources available to assist our heroes and their families and caregivers. The DoD Agency Plan seeks to increase awareness and understanding of these resources to better assist AAPI warriors and their families and caregivers as they successfully recover, rehabilitate, and reintegrate back into society.

Goal 2. ***Provide maximum practicable opportunity for AAPI small business participation in DoD acquisitions.***

The Department of Defense frequently accounts for a large portion of the entire federal government's procurement budget. The government-wide goal for participation by small businesses is at least 23 percent of the total value of all prime contract awards for each fiscal year. As a part of that goal, the DoD Agency Plan seeks to increase participation of AAPI small businesses in DoD acquisitions.

Goal 3. ***Foster the recruitment, career development, and advancement of AAPIs at the Department of Defense.***

One of the Initiative's key cross-cutting objectives is to foster the recruitment, career development, and advancement of AAPIs in the Federal Government. The DoD Agency Plan seeks to ensure that the Department of Defense meets that objective by increasing the number of AAPI applicants to entry-level, mission critical, and senior positions as well as by increasing AAPI applicants for Senior Executive Service positions.

Mission. The U.S. Department of Education (ED) seeks to promote student achievement and preparation for global competitiveness by fostering educational excellence and ensuring equal access.

President Obama's vision is that by 2020, America will again have the best-educated, most competitive workforce in the world with the highest proportion of college graduates of any country. To do this, the United States must also close the achievement gap, so that all youth — regardless of their backgrounds — graduate from high school ready to succeed in college and careers.

PRIORITY PROGRAM GOALS FOR THE ASIAN AMERICAN AND PACIFIC ISLANDER COMMUNITY

Per Executive Order 13515, ED has identified five high-priority goals that will span the next two years. These goals will help increase the AAPI community's participation in and access to the agency's programs.

Goal 1. *Identify and promote three models of disaggregated data systems that increase attainment for AAPI students and have the potential for national replication.*
A lack of disaggregated data for AAPI students leads to hidden achievement gaps that are barriers to raising student achievement. While educational attainment among East Asian and South Asian groups is generally high, educational attainment among Pacific Islanders and Southeast Asian groups is relatively low.

Goal 2. *Improve access and increase technical assistance and outreach to institutions that qualify for ED's Asian American and Native American Pacific Islander-Serving Institution (AANAPISI) program.*
ED's AANAPISI program supports eligible higher education institutions to increase self-sufficiency by improving academic programs, institutional management, and fiscal stability. AANAPISIs seek to increase participation and academic attainment of low income, high-need students, and serve communities with high poverty and high rates of limited English proficiency.

Goal 3. *Identify and promote three successful anti-bullying programs in schools, and disseminate anti-bullying information to AAPI community.*
Bullying is widespread in American schools, with more than 32 percent of U.S. school children saying they had been bullied by other students during the current term, according to a survey funded by the National Institute of Child Health and Human Development. This issue has particularly affected AAPI communities in recent years with high-profile school harassment incidents in several cities.

Goal 4. *Improve delivery of services to AAPI English learners (EL).*
Studies indicate that EL students are much less likely than other students to score at or above proficient levels in both mathematics and reading/language arts. Furthermore, EL students tend to go to public schools that have low standardized test scores. This goal aims to provide the support EL students need to be equally successful as non-EL students.

Goal 5. *Increase recruitment of AAPI teachers.*
While AAPIs comprise 3.9% of the total enrollment in public elementary and secondary schools, they represent only 1.5% of teachers. The gaps are greater in certain states. In California for example, 11.3% of students in elementary and secondary schools are AAPIs, yet only 4.9% of the teachers are AAPIs. This goal aims to recruit more teachers who are more representative of the national student population and who are trained to manage diverse student populations.

Mission. The U.S. Department of Energy (DOE) advances the national, economic, and energy security of the United States; promotes scientific and technological innovation in support of that mission; and ensures the environmental cleanup of the national nuclear weapons complex.

PRIORITY PROGRAM GOALS FOR THE ASIAN AMERICAN AND PACIFIC ISLANDER COMMUNITY

Per Executive Order 13515, the Department of Energy (DOE) has identified two high-priority goals that will span the next two years. These goals will help increase the AAPI community's participation in and access to the agency's programs.

Goal 1. *Increase outreach efforts to Asian American and Native Pacific Islander academic institutions to promote entry-level employment opportunities.*

As of September 30, 2010, Asian Americans and Pacific Islanders represented five percent of the total DOE workforce, .02 percent above the Relevant Civilian Labor Force, whose representation of Asian Americans is 4.8 percent. Asian men and women are equally represented at six percent of the employees in GS13/14/15 levels. Asian Americans represent 3.7 percent of the Senior Executive Service, of which 2.2 percent are women and 1.5 percent are men.

When analyzing diversity data of DOE Federal interns, Asians Americans/Pacific Islanders are well represented. They comprise 6.5 percent of the Federal interns hired from FY05–FY10. However, of the Asian American interns hired at the GS-11 pay scale, 80 percent were male, and of those hired at the GS-12, 100 percent were male.

Targeted recruitment efforts are needed to increase representation of all women minority groups, including Asian American women who qualify at the journeyman levels.

Goal 2. *Increase outreach and small business opportunities.*

The Federal Data Procurement System and the DOE's "Information Data Warehouse" capture small business awards to Asian Pacific American business ($36.2 million in Recovery Awards) and Sub-Continent Asian American ($11.9 million in Recovery Awards). While this data is comparable to other socio-economic business categories, more effort is needed to ensure that Asian American businesses are able to maximize opportunities available to small businesses.

Mission. The U.S. Department of Health and Human Services (HHS) enhances the health and well-being of Americans by providing for effective health and human services and by fostering sound, sustained advances in the sciences underlying medicine, public health, and social services.

Asian Americans and Pacific Islanders often receive inadequate care or suffer from poor health compared to white Americans. Tackling health disparities is a top priority for the Administration. To do this, root causes of health disparities must be addressed by examining the social determinants of health and the differences in access to health care while promoting prevention and public health.

PRIORITY PROGRAM GOALS FOR THE ASIAN AMERICAN AND PACIFIC ISLANDER COMMUNITY

Per Executive Order 13515, HHS has identified four high-priority goals that will span the next two years. These goals will help increase the AAPI community's participation in and access to the agency's programs.

Goal 1. *Prevent, treat and control Hepatitis B Viral (HBV) infections in AAPI communities.*
An estimated 3.5-5.3 million persons are living with viral hepatitis in the United States. Most that are infected remain unaware of their infection and therefore, do not receive care and treatment. About 1.25 million Americans are chronically infected with HBV, and AAPIs represent nearly half of these chronic HBV-infected persons in the U.S. If not treated, 15%-40% of persons living with viral hepatitis will develop liver cirrhosis or experience other conditions that affect the liver, including liver cancer. HHS convened a Viral Hepatitis Interagency Working Group that developed "Hepatitis and Liver Cancer: HHS Action Plan for Prevention and Treatment of Viral Hepatitis, 2011." The action plan will improve national coordination and collaboration for treatment, prevention and control of viral hepatitis, particularly HBV infections.

Goal 2. *Improve data collection in AAPI communities.*
The 2009 IOM report, "Race, Ethnicity, and Language Data: Standardization for Health Care Quality Improvement," recommends that in addition to the standard OMB classifications on race and ethnicity, more granular race/ethnicity information be collected to distinguish variations in health outcomes among different racial and ethnic subpopulation groups. Detailed data is a fundamental step in identifying which populations are most at risk and what specific interventions are most effective in attaining improved health care quality for specific populations.

Goal 3. *Increase AAPI health care workforce.*
The 2004 IOM report titled "In the Nation's Compelling Interest: Ensuring Diversity in the Health Care Workforce," recommends the need to increase diversity in the health professions in the U.S. because of the rapid demographic changes with increase in non-white populations and those with limited English proficiency. The IOM reports that the new underrepresented minorities in the health professions include subpopulations of AAPIs. The 2010 Association of American Medical Colleges Diversity in Physician Workforce report indicates that 12.8% are Asian Americans and only 0.5% are American Indians/Alaskan Natives. NHPI physicians are included in the AI/NA category. Data from various studies document that AAPI patients confront cultural and linguistic barriers in health care, resulting in worsening clinical outcomes. HHS will support increasing the pipeline of AANHPI health professionals.

Goal 4. *Improve health conditions and access to health care services by Native Hawaiians and Pacific Islanders.*
The NHPI health insurance coverage rate is lower than most other racial and ethnic groups in the U.S. In 2008, one in four NHPIs under 65 years of age was uninsured. Diabetes, cancer, cardiovascular diseases hypertension and infant mortality are major health issues among NHPIs. NHPI adults and adolescents have disproportionately high levels of mental health problems. According to the 2007 Youth Risk Behavior Survey, about a quarter of NHPI adolescents had attempted suicide. These health problems are compounded by obesity, lack of healthy lifestyles, lack of extended family support systems, and lack of culturally competent health professionals. The Plan addresses the main health issues that impact NHPIs.

Mission. The U.S. Department of Homeland Security (DHS) leads the United States efforts to ensure a homeland that is safe, secure, and resilient against terrorism and other hazards where American interests, aspirations, and way of life can thrive.

PRIORITY PROGRAM GOALS FOR THE ASIAN AMERICAN AND PACIFIC ISLANDER COMMUNITY

Per Executive Order 13515, DHS has identified three high-priority goals that will span the next two years. These goals will help increase the AAPI community's participation in and access to the agency's programs. If these projects are successful, they will serve as pilot projects to reach other communities within the population that DHS serves.

Goal 1. ***Ensure resilience from disasters by reducing cultural and language barriers that hinder AAPI and other immigrant communities during disaster response and the post-disaster recovery phase.***
DHS, through our component FEMA, takes a lead federal role in preparing for, responding to and assisting communities to recover from natural and manmade disasters. With the support of both FEMA and the DHS Office for Civil Rights and Civil Liberties, we strive to overcome hurdles that make it harder for segments of the community to respond in an emergency. Language and culture can become barriers to AAPI and other immigrant communities in emergency response (like evacuation orders) and access to recovery programs. By studying a few key geographic locations where there is a high concentration of AAPI immigrants and recurring natural disasters, DHS plans to develop and report on best practices that bridge language and cultural barriers.

Goal 2. ***Strengthen the homeland security enterprise by reducing language barriers to AAPI access to DHS programs and agencies generally.***
DHS plans to implement Limited English Proficiency programs throughout DHS, particularly with reference to major AAPIs languages.

Goal 3. ***Administer our immigration laws better by increasing communication between U.S. Citizenship and Immigration Services (USCIS) field offices and AAPI-serving organizations to better inform the AAPI community about the immigration process and opportunities to engage with USCIS, and to better inform USCIS about specific needs in the AAPI community.***
Asian and Pacific Islander immigrants constitute a large number of the new citizens processed by USCIS every year. By increasing opportunities for AAPI-serving organizations and USCIS headquarters and field offices to learn from each other and work together, DHS will better administer our immigration laws with greater understanding of the specific needs of the AAPI community. As part of this increased outreach, USCIS will continue to inform AAPI-serving organizations about opportunities to compete for the 2011 Citizenship and Integration Grants.

Mission. The Department of Housing and Urban Development (HUD) creates strong, sustainable, inclusive communities and quality affordable homes for all.

HUD is working to strengthen the housing market to bolster the economy and protect consumers; meet the need for quality affordable rental homes; utilize housing as a platform for improving quality of life; build inclusive and sustainable communities free from discrimination; and transform the way HUD does business.

PRIORITY PROGRAM GOALS FOR THE ASIAN AMERICAN AND PACIFIC ISLANDER COMMUNITY

Per Executive Order 13515, HUD has identified five high-priority goals that will span the next two years. These goals will help increase the AAPI community's participation in and access to the agency's programs.

Goal 1. *Increase the AAPI community's access to federal funding.*
HUD plans to create a streamlined process to ensure that appropriate funding opportunities reach the AAPI community by 2012. This can be accomplished by, among other actions, partnering with Asian American and Native American Pacific Islander Serving Institutions (AANAPISIs) and incorporating language into funding competitions to encourage the inclusion of minority communities.

Goal 2. *Increase the number of AAPIs with access to linguistically appropriate resources.*
HUD will seek to increase the number of programs that provide linguistically appropriate resources to the AAPI community. Thus far, HUD has translated over 100 vital documents into 16 different languages, including Khmer (official language of Cambodia), Chinese, Korean, Tagalog, and Vietnamese. In addition, HUD's Open Government Plan includes a language line that provides translation into over 100 languages.

HUD will continue to identify agency materials that reach an AAPI audience and monitor to ensure that materials are culturally and linguistically appropriate. HUD will also seek to ensure that key HUD documents are translated into appropriate AAPI languages and distributed to the AAPI community.

Goal 3. *Foster the recruitment, career development and advancement of AAPIs in the Federal Government.*
HUD plans to accomplish this goal by increasing the number of AAPI applicants to the federal government; increasing the awareness of AAPIs about and applications from AAPI's to innovative internship, fellowship, and work-study programs; increasing recruitment and leadership opportunities for AAPIs; and strengthening its diversity and affirmative employment measures.

Goal 4. *Improve federal civil rights protections for the AAPI community.*
HUD will rigorously enforce civil rights statutes/laws that require equal access and non-discrimination in federal programs that involve grants, loans, contracts, financial aid and other benefits. HUD will accomplish this goal by evaluating trends and patterns of compliance and enforcement activity (e.g., fair housing, contract compliance, environmental justice, etc.) for AAPI populations and subpopulations. HUD will also conduct expanded outreach with and develop partnerships with AA/NHPI community serving organizations to publicize enforcement processes and programs.

Goal 5. *Improve the data collected on AAPIs in each program.*
Depending on the availability of funds, HUD plans to conduct an evaluation of the impact of foreclosures on the AAPI community. HUD is working to disaggregate data by the categories laid out in OMB Directive 15, for all major programs, including: home ownership, tenant based rental assistance, and public housing.

Mission. The U.S. Department of the Interior (DOI) protects America's natural resources and heritage, honors our cultures and tribal communities, and supplies the energy to power our future. Our mission is as simple as it is profound. Interior protects America's natural resources and cultural heritage. Interior's land and community-based programs touch the lives of most Americans, including 1.7 million American Indians and Alaska Natives.

We are the Department of America. We work for the people of this country from sea to shining sea, from the Everglades to Yosemite, from Glacier National Park in Montana to the islands of Samoa and Guam and the Virgin Islands. And as the Department of America, our ranks must begin to reflect the face of the American public we serve.

PRIORITY PROGRAM GOALS FOR THE ASIAN AMERICAN AND PACIFIC ISLANDER COMMUNITY

Per Executive Order 13515, DOI has identified five high-priority goals that will span the next two years. These goals will help increase the AAPI community's participation in and access to the agency's programs.

Goal 1. Increase participation of AAPIs in DOI's mission-critical occupations.
The Department will work to increase the number AAPI applicants for employment by advertising its job announcements in AAPI communities and newspapers, sharing employment opportunities with AAPI organizations, and providing training for managers on flexible hiring authorities that increase opportunities to employ college graduates.

Goal 2. Increase DOI's capacity to disseminate information and share ideas with AAPI communities and organizations.
Interior will implement customer engagement software and utilize it to engage AAPI serving institutions and organizations to ensure that information regarding opportunities to participate in Interior programs reach AAPI communities. This software will also provide a pathway for ideas from AAPI communities to reach Interior.

Goal 3. Improve Federal civil rights protections for the AAPI community.
Interior will rigorously enforce civil rights laws that require equal access and non-discrimination in federal programs that involve grants, loans, contracts, financial aid and other benefits. The Department will evaluate trends and patterns of compliance and enforcement activity for AAPI population and subpopulations; generate a report of findings and recommendations; and develop an action plan.

Goal 4. Prepare Senior Executives to lead efforts to create a strong culture of diversity and inclusion at DOI.
Interior will hold a leadership summit for all Senior Executives to educate Senior Executives about diversity and inclusion and to communicate leadership expectations; teach them how to use multiple cultural backgrounds as competitive tools; and prepare them for emerging workforce trends such as growing competition for America's best talent.

Goal 5. Support indigenous renewable energy strategy in the insular areas.
Interior will conduct Renewable and Energy Efficiency Summits with insular area leaders to encourage the leadership to make renewable energy a priority, and to connect leaders with federal opportunities to grow renewable energy initiatives in the insular areas.

Mission. The U.S. Department of Justice (DOJ) seeks to enforce the law and defend the interests of the United States according to the law; to ensure public safety against threats foreign and domestic; to provide federal leadership in preventing and controlling crime; to seek just punishment for those guilty of unlawful behavior; and to ensure fair and impartial administration of justice for all Americans.

PRIORITY PROGRAM GOALS FOR THE ASIAN AMERICAN AND PACIFIC ISLANDER COMMUNITY

Per Executive Order 13515, DOJ has identified five high-priority goals that will span the next two years. These goals will help increase the AAPI community's participation in and access to the agency's programs.

Goal 1. *Reduce Language Barriers to AAPI Access of Federal Programs/Agencies.*
Pursuant to Executive Order 13166, "Improving Access to Services for Persons with Limited English Proficiency," DOJ coordinates federal agency implementation plans to ensure that limited English proficiency (LEP) individuals can access the agencies' federally conducted programs. The Attorney General has created a working group to have each component create its own language access plan, to identify LEP needs and gaps in service, and to create component language access plans.

Goal 2. *Ensure that the Federal Government is Properly Assessing and Addressing Hate Crimes and Other Crimes in the Asian American and Pacific Islander ("AAPI") Community.*
DOJ will continue to build on a 2009 Bureau of Justice Statistics report devoted to the study of victimization amongst AAPIs by distributing the report widely to inform the public about crime in AAPI communities and identifying the number of AAPI victims served by Office on Violence Against Women grantees. DOJ's Community Oriented Policing Services will highlight the needs of underserved communities, including AAPIs, in its discretionary grant program and solicit grant proposals from these communities. The Civil Rights Division will work to identify and prosecute hate crimes against AAPIs where the facts warrant.

Goal 3. *Protect AAPI Women from Domestic Violence.*
DOJ's Office on Violence Against Women (OVW) is responsible for implementing the Violence Against Women Act's (VAWA) "Culturally and Linguistically Specific Services Program" and will support the development of innovative culturally and linguistically specific strategies and projects to enhance access to services and resources for victims of violence against women. In FY 2011, OVW will highlight the needs of immigrant and LEP communities, including the AAPI community, in its grant programs and its outreach and will assess various programs' support levels of AAPI-focused organizations.

Goal 4. *Enhance Efforts to Combat Human Trafficking.*
DOJ will expand upon its coordination efforts within DOJ and with other federal agencies to enhance federal investigations and prosecutions of human trafficking. DOJ seeks to ensure that efforts to fight human trafficking are comprehensive and culturally competent by, among other things, accepting referrals from 24-hour human trafficking hotlines and funding culturally competent, comprehensive services to victims of human trafficking.

Goal 5. *Enhance the Protection of Civil Rights of Vulnerable AAPI Immigrant Populations.*
For FY 2011, "Reinvigorate Federal Civil Rights Enforcement" has been identified by the Attorney General as a high priority performance goal for DOJ. DOJ's Civil Rights Division will continue to engage in outreach to immigrant communities and underserved groups, including AAPIs, to ensure that they know their rights and the government services available to them. DOJ's Civil Rights Division also will continue to revitalize the National Origin Working Group to facilitate the delivery of services to underserved immigrant populations. In addition, DOJ will enhance the language and legal orientation services it offers to immigrant populations, including AAPIs, such as the provision of language interpreters at all immigration court proceedings to parties who need an interpreter.

Mission. The U.S. Department of Labor (DOL) fosters, promotes, and develops the welfare of the wage earners, job seekers, and retirees of the United States; improves working conditions; advances opportunities for profitable employment; and assures work-related benefits and rights.

DOL is committed to assisting all communities, including Asian American and Pacific Islanders (AAPIs), through the Secretary's simple and straightforward vision of *Good Jobs for Everyone*. Agencies within the Department of Labor are individually and collectively directing resources and efforts to reach out to the most vulnerable and hard-to-reach workers across the country, including members of the AAPI community.

Priority Program Goals for the Asian American and Pacific Islander Community

Per Executive Order 13515, DOL has identified five high-priority goals that will span the next two years. These goals will help increase the AAPI community's participation in and access to the agency's programs.

Goal 1. *Prepare workers for good jobs and ensure fair compensation.*
The Employment and Training Administration (ETA) will conduct a baseline assessment of AAPI participation in its job training and employment-related services in order to identify areas for increased participation of AAPIs. Also, in order to narrow "wage income inequality," the Civil Rights Center (CRC) will increase efforts necessary to identify systemic discrimination against protected groups, including AAPIs, in the workforce development system.

Goal 2. *Ensure workplaces are safe and healthful.*
In an effort to educate the most vulnerable and hard-to-reach workers, including AAPIs, the Occupational Safety and Health Administration (OSHA) will foster local partnerships and working relationships with employers, workers, and organizations that represent AAPI workers in high hazard industries. In addition, OSHA will coordinate regional summits and meetings targeting AAPI workers and employers.

Goal 3. *Assure fair and high quality work-life environments.*
In order to ensure fair and diverse workplaces, the Office of Federal Contract Compliance (OFCCP) will increase awareness of the laws that prohibit employment discrimination by federal contractors system among AAPIs and all workers through an education campaign, including the production of worker's rights materials, outreach at community events, and engaging AAPI leaders as stakeholders in OFCCP's enforcement and regulatory efforts.

Goal 4. *Secure health benefits, and for those not working, provide income security*.
In an effort to improve health benefits and retirement security, the Employee Benefits Security Administration (EBSA) will educate AAPIs, and the general public, on employment-based retirement security and health plan benefits. To do so, EBSA will conduct briefings with organizations that serve AAPIs, including local community centers and business organizations.

Goal 5. *Produce timely and accurate data on the economic conditions of workers and their families.*
Through its regular release of statistics from the Current Population Survey, the Bureau of Labor Statistics (BLS) will advance relevant, evidence-based research on labor market activity, working conditions, and price changes in the economy for the workplace as a whole, including AAPIs.

Mission. The U.S. Department of State advances freedom for the benefit of the American people and the international community by helping to build and sustain a more democratic, secure, and prosperous world composed of well-governed states that respond to the needs of their people, reduce widespread poverty, and act responsibly within the international system.

The Secretary of State is responsible for ensuring equal opportunity in the Department. The Secretary has delegated this authority to the Director of the Office of Civil Rights (S/OCR), who also serves as the Department's Chief Diversity Officer. Operational responsibility for compliance with Department policies and programs lies with the Department's line managers.

PRIORITY PROGRAM GOALS FOR THE ASIAN AMERICAN AND PACIFIC ISLANDER COMMUNITY

Per Executive Order 13515, the Department has identified two high-priority goals that will span the next two years. These goals will help increase the AAPI community's participation in and access to the agency's programs.

Goal 1. Foster the recruitment, career development and advancement of AAPIs in the Department of State.
The Department engages in an aggressive recruitment and outreach program to achieve a diverse workforce; however, Asian Americans and Pacific Islanders are underrepresented in the senior ranks of the Civil and Foreign Service. The steps below will address this challenge.

- Continue to increase AAPI applicants to the DOS.
- Continue to promote participation of AAPIs in innovative internship, fellowship, and work-study programs.
- Address lack of AAPIs in Senior Executive Service (SES) and Senior Foreign Service (SFS).
- Address retention of AAPI employees.
- Develop and include diversity measures as critical elements in executive and management performance plans.

Goal 2. Increase the number of AAPIs with access to linguistically appropriate resources.
This goal addresses Executive Order 13166, which requires all agencies to ensure that people with limited English proficiency have meaningful access to an agency's information and resources. Below are the Department's goals and major steps necessary to them.

- Confer with Department of Justice Coordination and Review Section to evaluate status of agency plan related to Executive Order 13166 Improving Access to Services for Persons with Limited English Proficiency.
- Identify agency materials that reach an AAPI audience and monitor to ensure that materials are culturally and linguistically appropriate.

Mission. The U.S. Department of Transportation (DOT) serves the United States by ensuring a fast, safe, efficient, accessible and convenient transportation system that meets our vital national interests and enhances the quality of life of the American people, today and into the future, and promote more livable communities through sustainable surface transportation programs. The American public and state departments of transportation are the Agency's primary customers.

PRIORITY GOALS FOR THE ASIAN AMERICAN AND PACIFIC ISLANDER COMMUNITY

Per Executive Order 13515, DOT has identified five high-priority goals that will span the next two years. These goals will help increase the AAPI community's participation in and access to the agency's programs.

Goal 1. ***Increase participation from the AAPI community on key areas related to Department of Transportation policies and programs.***
DOT is improving the livability of our Nation's communities by making transportation a more integral part of our communities. A strategic communication plan will ensure that that these goals will be communicated to AAPI communities nationwide.

Goal 2. ***Increase the AAPI community's access to DOT's Disadvantaged Business Enterprise opportunities.***
A strategic marketing plan will ensure that funding opportunities reach the appropriate AAPI communities.

Goal 3. ***Promote messages to the AAPI communities about DOT's Safety Campaigns.***
Improving safety and promoting livable communities are top priorities for DOT. One of DOT's high-priority goals is to reduce the rate of highway fatalities. DOT is championing a safety culture in our Nation and encouraging our partners, stakeholders, and the public to redouble their efforts to reduce transportation-related fatalities and injuries and make our Nation's transportation system the safest in the world.

Goal 4. ***Foster the recruitment, career development, and advancement of AAPIs in the Federal Government.***
To maximize its effectiveness, DOT seeks to achieve a diverse and inclusive workforce. DOT is committed to analyzing its workplace policies, practices and procedures to ensure equal employment opportunities for applicants and employees.

Goal 5. ***Partner with Asian American and Native American Pacific Islanders Serving Institutions (AANAPISI)***
The AANAPISI program supports eligible higher education institutions to increase self-sufficiency by improving academic programs, institutional management, and fiscal stability. DOT seeks to increase participation in internship programs by recruiting students attending the AANAPISI program.

Mission. The U.S. Department of the Treasury (Treasury) serves the American people by strengthening the U.S. economy, supporting job creation, and restoring confidence in the financial system.

Priority Program Goals for the Asian American and Pacific Islander Community

Per Executive Order 13515, Treasury has identified five high-priority goals that will span the next two years. These goals will help increase the AAPI community's participation in and access to the agency's programs.

Goal 1.   *Maintain and enhance level of participation of Asian American and Pacific Islanders (AAPI) in mission critical positions at Treasury.*

Goal 2.   *Increase awareness of career development, leadership, and advancement opportunities among Treasury employees.*

Goal 3.   *Increase number of limited English proficient individuals, including AAPIs, with access to information about Treasury programs.*

Goal 4.   *Ensure departmental outreach plans focusing on Small and Disadvantaged Businesses (SDBs) include components targeting SDBs owned by or servicing AAPI communities.*

Goal 5.   *Enhance outreach efforts to underserved communities, including AAPIs, regarding relevant Treasury programs.*

Mission. The Department of Veterans Affairs (VA) is responsible for a timeless mission: "To care for him who shall have borne the battle, and for his widow, and his orphan"— by serving and honoring the men and women who are America's Veterans.

President Obama has repeatedly shown his support for military Veterans through initiatives such as the Veterans Health Care Budget Reform and Transparency Act as well as showing his support for military members and Veterans.

PRIORITY PROGRAM GOALS FOR THE ASIAN AMERICAN AND PACIFIC ISLANDER COMMUNITY

Per Executive Order 13515, the VA has identified four high-priority goals that will span the next two years. These goals will help increase the AAPI community's participation in and access to the agency's programs.

Goal 1. *In conjunction with HUD, reduce the homeless veteran population to 59,000 by June 2012 on the way to eliminating veteran homelessness.*
> In recent decades, the number of homeless Veterans has steadily increased. Today, there are an estimated 107,000 homeless Veterans. The Department of Veterans Affairs (VA) is taking decisive action to end Veteran homelessness in five years. All Veterans at risk for homelessness or attempting to exit homelessness must have easy access to programs and services. VA offers a variety of resources, programs, and benefits such as prevention services, housing support services, treatment, job training, and other services to address this challenge.

Goal 2. *Improve the quality, access, and value of health care, including mental health care, provided to AAPI Veterans.*
> The VA's primary mission is to care for and provide benefits and services to military Veterans. As such, VA provides medical benefits packages to eligible military Veterans. VA continually seeks to improve services and increase Veteran awareness of such services and benefits. VA maintains highly qualified health and mental health care professionals to provide these services. These services and benefits are increasingly in more demand as many Veterans are recent returnees from Iraq and Afghanistan, with many of them belonging to AAPI communities. Therefore, it is pertinent for the VA to reach out to those Veterans to educate them on available services and benefits.

Goal 3. *Foster the recruitment, career development and advancement of AAPIs in the VA.*
> VA is constantly seeking highly qualified professionals and employees to develop into those positions. As part of this mission, VA seeks to increase AAPI applicants to VA career opportunities; internally increase participation rate of AAPIs in innovative internship, fellowship, and work-study programs; increase applicants for Senior Executive Service positions; develop and include diversity and affirmative employment measures as critical elements in executive and management performance plans; and implement training to educate AAPI employees on the available leadership, career development, and educational programs.

Goal 4. *Increase awareness and access to health services for AAPI Veterans in rural areas.*
> About 3 million Veterans enrolled in the VA Health Care System live in rural or highly rural areas of the country. Men and women Veterans from geographically rural areas make up a disproportionate share of service members and comprise about 39% of the enrolled Veterans who served in Iraq and Afghanistan; many of who are returning to their rural communities. In order to better serve rural Veterans, the VA created the Office of Rural Health in 2006. VA seeks to increase outreach, health and mental health services, and increase awareness of other benefits and services to ensure Veterans in rural areas receive proper services and benefits.

Mission. The U.S. Environmental Protection Agency (EPA) protects human health and the environment. The Agency ensures that all Americans are protected from significant risks due to environmental factors, such as air and water pollution, toxic chemicals, and hazardous waste where they live, learn, and work.

PRIORITY PROGRAM GOALS FOR THE ASIAN AMERICAN AND PACIFIC ISLANDER COMMUNITY

Per Executive Order 13515, EPA has identified four high-priority goals that will span the next two years. These goals will help increase the AAPI community's participation in and access to the agency's programs.

Goal 1. ***Build Effective Partnership with AAPI Organizations to Improve the Environment and Economic Development for AAPIs Communities.***

The Agency is working with AAPI organizations to improve the environment and public health for these communities while encouraging economic opportunities through those efforts. EPA efforts include increased information on funding opportunities and providing technical assistance in the Brownfield programs, conducting outreach efforts on chemical exposure to nail salon workers, engaging dry cleaners in best management practices and safer alternatives in relevant regions, educating the AAPI communities about contaminated fish, and providing infrastructure support for wastewater and drinking water facilities in Hawaii and Pacific Island Territories.

Goal 2. ***Increase Environmental Outreach and Information to AAPIs.***

The Agency recognizes the need to increase environmental awareness in the AAPI community through appropriate outreach including information written in the appropriate AAPI language. As part of this effort the EPA website includes portals with environmental information in Chinese, Vietnamese and Korean. To help community members better understand the cleanup process, appropriate Superfund and Brownfield outreach materials will be translated into Chinese, Vietnamese, and Laotian.

The EPA's guide to *"Protecting the Health of Nail Salon Workers"* has been translated into Vietnamese and Korean. In 2011, EPA will be conducting a series of Train-the-Trainer workshops to educate nail salon workers on chemical safety and greening their business.

We will reach out to the communities to increase AAPI participation via the annual national environmental justice conference where we will raise awareness on AAPI environmental challenges to all participants. To ensure full participation, EPA advocates will conduct environmental justice listening sessions in the AAPI communities and engage communities in decision-making processes.

Goal 3. ***Improve Employment Opportunities and Career Advancement for AAPIs in the EPA Workforce.***

EPA has made significant progress in attracting AAPI professionals to the Agency and is committed to increasing the information on career opportunities to AAPIs. This effort includes programs to both encourage the participation of AAPIs in EPA's workforce as well as in career development opportunities. Further outreach initiatives geared specifically to AAPI are also being developed.

Goal 4. ***Create a partnership and promote awareness of resources available for Asian American and Native American Pacific Islander Serving Institutions (AANAPISIs) in order to promote environmental education and create an education pipeline.***

AANAPISIs seek to increase the participation and academic attainment of low income, high-need students, and serve communities with high poverty and high rates of limited English proficiency. EPA will endeavor to strategically partner with AANAPISIs, to increase both environmental awareness as well as highlighting the myriad of EPA's mission critical occupations that they can strive for. The AANAPISIs partnership can be a vital contributor in promoting economic opportunities while strongly touting the necessary environmental protections which positively impact communities throughout the country. This will reinforce America's competitiveness in the global arena.

Mission. The U.S. Equal Employment Opportunity Commission (EEOC) promotes equality of opportunity in the workplace and enforces federal laws prohibiting employment discrimination.

The Commission receives, investigates, and resolves charges of employment discrimination filed against private sector employers, employment agencies, labor unions, and state and local governments. The Commission may also file employment discrimination suits in court. The EEOC also leads and coordinates equal employment opportunity efforts across the federal government, and conducts administrative hearings and issues appellate decisions on complaints of discrimination filed by federal employees and applicants for federal employment. Finally, the Commission engages in extensive communication and outreach, provides technical assistance, and promulgates regulations and written enforcement guidance to help employers, employees, and potential employees better understand their rights and responsibilities under the laws the EEOC enforces.

Priority Program Goals for the Asian American and Pacific Islander Community

Per Executive Order 13515, the EEOC has identified five high-priority goals that will span the next two years. These goals will help increase the AAPI community's participation in and access to the agency's programs.

Goal 1. *Improve data collection and analysis regarding AAPIs and other underserved populations.*
To better understand the populations the EEOC serves, the EEOC will assess whether new AAPI national origin categories should be added in current data collections, improve its analysis of the AAPI workforce and charge data, and improve its dissemination of these types of data to the public. Lack of disaggregated data obscures the differences and needs between individual AAPI communities.

Goal 2. *Increase and improve the EEOC's communication with various AAPI communities to ensure that AAPIs and other underserved populations can fully utilize the services of the EEOC.*
In fiscal year 2010, AAPIs filed 3% of the almost 100,000 charges of employment discrimination filed with the EEOC against private employers. Through conducting additional outreach activities, forming partnerships and relationships with AAPI organizations and media, and increasing access to linguistically appropriate resources and staff, the EEOC will help eliminate barriers to AAPIs reporting employment discrimination, such as a lack of awareness of their rights, limited English ability, fear or discomfort of dealing with a government agency, and cultural differences.

Goal 3. *Increase litigation and enforcement efforts of employment discrimination statutes enforced by the EEOC related to issues that significantly impact AAPIs such as race and national origin discrimination.*
For the last decade, the EEOC, on average, filed 370 employment discrimination cases a year. These cases arise in large part through the charges received from the general public. To ensure that the EEOC brings litigation involving issues that impact the AAPI community, the EEOC will ensure that it generates charges from the AAPI community, coordinates with other agencies, conducts training, and raises awareness about the importance of these issues with EEOC offices.

Goal 4. *Ensure that the EEOC is an inclusive workplace for all AAPIs to reach their full potential.*
The EEOC strives to be a model workplace. Increasing the applicant pool of qualified AAPIs, particularly for supervisory and Senior Executive Service positions, and focusing on recruitment, retention, and training will ensure that AAPIs have equal opportunity to compete for vacancies at the agency.

Goal 5. *Help ensure that the federal government is an inclusive workplace for all AAPIs to reach their full potential.*
While AAPIs comprise 5.8% of the federal workforce, they still face barriers to equal employment. The EEOC will continue to provide leadership, guidance, and technical support to federal agencies on all aspects of the federal government's equal employment opportunity program, including identifying the specific barriers AAPIs face and best practices for removing those barriers.

Mission. The U.S. Office of Personnel Management (OPM) recruits, retains, and honors a world-class workforce to serve the American people.

Our goal is to assist agencies as they hire the best, respect the workforce, expect the best, and honor service by leading the way in making the Federal government the model employer. Moreover, as the principal government agency charged with overseeing the merit-based civil service, OPM is working with other agencies to establish the Federal workforce as a government of the people, by the people and for the people that fully embraces the diversity of our people.

PRIORITY PROGRAM GOALS FOR THE ASIAN AMERICAN AND PACIFIC ISLANDER COMMUNITY

Per Executive Order 13515, OPM has identified two high-priority goals that will span the next two years. These goals will help increase the AAPI community's participation in and access to the agency's programs.

Goal 1. ***Increase the recruitment, career development and advancement of AAPIs in the Federal Government.***
Currently, AAPIs represent 6.29% of the Federal workforce, with the majority on AAPIs in GS-14 and GS-15 positions. However, AAPIs represent 2.84% of the Senior Executive Services (SES), 3.27% of First-level managers, 3.28% of Mid-level managers, and 4.47% in the Senior-level managers. This goal aims to increase the number of AAPIs in SES, supervisory and management selection pools, as well as increase agencies' use of succession planning.

Goal 2. ***Increase the recruitment, career development and advancement of AAPIs in the U.S. Office of Personnel Management.***
OPM must lead by example. AAPIs represent 6.29% of the Federal workforce; however, they represent 3.08% of OPM's workforce. Similarly, AAPI representation in the OPM workforce is lower than expected at the SES, supervisory and management level based upon their participation in the overall workforce. For OPM to lead, we must effectively implement our own initiatives and identify areas in which we can fully engage our employees.

Mission. The U.S. Social Security Administrations (SSA) delivers Social Security services that meet the changing needs of the public.

Priority Program Goals for the Asian American and Pacific Islander Community

Per Executive Order 13515, the Social Security Administration has identified four high-priority goals that will span the next two years. These goals will help increase the AAPI community's participation in and access to the agency's programs.

Goal 1. *Increase Understanding of Social Security Programs among AAPIs*

When applying for and receiving benefits, AAPIs may have trouble because of a lack of understanding of program benefits due to language and cultural barriers. We will enhance our national outreach efforts to the AAPI community to promote our programs and services.

Goal 2. *Foster the Recruitment, Career Development, and Advancement of AAPIs within the Agency*

AAPIs make up over 5% of our total workforce. We will continue to offer career development training and resources. We will participate in national/regional job fairs designed to recruit AAPI candidates at all levels. We will collaborate with our agency's Pacific Asian American Advisory Council to establish/increase participation of AAPIs in national career development programs.

Goal 3. *Increase Employees' Cultural and Linguistic Awareness about AAPIs*

We will improve our employees' awareness of AAPI culture and languages in order to enhance our services to the AAPI community.

Goal 4. *Enhance the services we currently provide the AAPIs community.*

We are committed to providing excellent service through a variety of channels, including telephone, field and hearing offices, and online. Our network of 1,300 field offices, interpreter services in over 150 languages and dialects (through the National Telephone Interpreter Service), and expansion of online services will contribute to the overall enhancement of service to AAPIs.

Mission. The National Aeronautics and Space Administration (NASA) drives advances in science, technology, and exploration to enhance knowledge, education, innovation, economic vitality, and stewardship of Earth.

The President's vision is that by 2020, America will again have the best-educated, most competitive workforce in the world with the highest proportion of college graduates of any country. To do this, the United States must also close the achievement gap, so that all youth — regardless of their backgrounds — graduate from high school ready to succeed in college and careers.

PRIORITY PROGRAM GOALS FOR THE ASIAN AMERICAN AND PACIFIC ISLANDER COMMUNITY

Per Executive Order 13515, NASA has identified four high-priority goals that will span the next two years. These goals will help increase the AAPI community's participation in and access to the agency's programs.

Goal 1. *Increase AAPI Diversity/Representation in the NASA workforce.*

NASA found that it has not effectively developed its recruitment strategies, succession management pipelines, leadership development initiatives, or mentoring programs to fully include AAPIs. One result has been a lower than expected representation of AAPIs in aerospace technology (AST) positions, both in entry-level and higher grade levels. Therefore, NASA will increase the participation of AAPIs in the NASA workforce, both in entry-level and high level positions.

Goal 2. *Increase the participation of AAPIs in NASA's education and research opportunities.*

Based on a host of research literature in the diversity and inclusion field that indicates heterogeneous work groups are more successful than homogenous ones, NASA believes that a more demographically diverse workforce, as well as a more inclusive work environment, one that encourages diverse inputs in arriving at the best technical solutions, will serve the NASA mission and help the agency to maintain its preeminence in the world economy. For these reasons, NASA seeks to expand the diversity of its workforce by increasing the participation of AAPIs in Science and Engineering occupations at the Agency and national level.

Goal 3. *Improve Outreach on NASA Business Opportunities with AAPI within the Small Business Community.*

NASA found a low participation of AAPIs in NASA Business Opportunities. Therefore, the agency will increase Small Business and Small and Disadvantaged Business conference participation of the AAPI business community, and will advise AAPI-owned small businesses on business opportunities and events.

Goal 4. *Better ensure meaningful access for AAPIs to programs and activities receiving NASA financial assistance.*

NASA's regulations under Title VI of the Civil Rights Act of 1964, which prohibits discrimination based on race, color, or national origin (including limited English proficiency, or LEP), require NASA to conduct civil rights compliance reviews of its grant recipient institutions to ensure that grantees are not discriminating on these bases and are providing equal opportunities for the beneficiaries of such grants. NASA grantees include universities and colleges, museums, science centers, and research institutes. These grantees are spread across the country, some of them in geographical areas with high AAPI populations. Consistent with NASA Title VI implementing regulations and LEP requirements and guidance, NASA conducts a fully-realized program of Title VI-LEP compliance reviews to ensure that national origin minorities, including AAPIs are not discriminated against in NASA funded programs, especially those serving the general public. Therefore, by the end of FY 2012, NASA will conduct at least one civil rights compliance review under Title VI-LEP at a NASA grant recipient institution located in an area with a large AAPI population, with appropriate findings and recommendations to ensure meaningful access to LEP AAPI populations.

Mission. The mission of the Corporation for National and Community Service (CNCS), a federal agency, is to improve lives, strengthen communities, and foster civic engagement through service and volunteering. Through AmeriCorps, Learn and Serve America and Senior Corps and our other programs and activities, five million Americans serve with nearly 70,000 organizations in the national service network.

Our primary role is to provide critical resources and leadership to support local initiatives that tackle community challenges in six focus areas: disaster services, economic opportunity, education, environmental stewardship, healthy futures, and veterans and military families. CNCS adds further value through our focus on the quality of the service participant's experience and continued engagement.

PRIORITY PROGRAM GOALS FOR THE ASIAN AMERICAN AND PACIFIC ISLANDER COMMUNITY

Per Executive Order 13515, CNCS has identified four high-priority goals that will span the next two years. These goals will help increase the AAPI community's participation in and access to the agency's programs.

Goal 1. ***Increase the impact of national service on community needs in communities served by CNCS-supported programs.***
Our belief is that Americans can effectively respond to challenges by getting involved in their local communities through service, and that citizen-centered action can drive community solutions. CNCS provides funding to address the needs of underserved communities, including AAPIs, with a priority for education, veterans, and military families.

Goal 2. ***Strengthen national service so that participants engaged in CNCS-supported programs consistently find satisfaction, meaning, and opportunity.***
The national service experience offers a unique combination of professional, educational and life benefits to service participants. CNCS will continue to expand our reach to include more Americans of diverse backgrounds – including AAPIs – so that they may take full advantage of the distinct benefits of service and develop a sustained commitment to civic engagement and national service.

Goal 3. ***Maximize the value we add to grantees, partners, and participants.***
CNCS seeks to strengthen the collective capacity of the agency and the national service network to measure performance and conduct rigorous evaluations of programs, many of which serve and engage AAPI communities. This knowledge base of best practices will provide organizations in our network with tools to better achieve desired results and measure their performance. CNCS also serves as a catalyst for leveraging federal resources with private funding and local collaboration with philanthropies, organizations, and institutions of higher education familiar with the AAPI community.

Goal 4. ***Fortify management operations and sustain a capable, responsive, and accountable organization.***
CNCS is optimally positioned to meet the strategic goals and objectives listed above by building on our current infrastructure, especially through human capital efforts. As such, CNCS seeks to increase the application rate of AAPIs applying to volunteer at the agency, and develop and promote diversity and affirmative employment measures that protect the rights of a diverse staff.

EXECUTIVE ORDER

INCREASING PARTICIPATION OF ASIAN AMERICANS AND PACIFIC ISLANDERS IN FEDERAL PROGRAMS

By the authority vested in me as President by the Constitution and the laws of the United States of America, it is hereby ordered as follows:

Section 1. Policy. The more than 16 million Asian Americans and Pacific Islanders (AAPIs) across our country have helped build a strong and vibrant America. The AAPI communities represent many ethnicities and languages that span generations, and their shared achievements are an important part of the American experience. They have started businesses and generated jobs, including founding some of our Nation's most successful and innovative enterprises. The AAPI communities have made important contributions to science and technology, culture and the arts, and the professions, including business, law, medicine, education, and politics.

While we acknowledge the many contributions of the AAPI communities to our Nation, we also recognize the challenges still faced by many AAPIs. Of the more than a million AAPI-owned businesses, many firms are small sole-proprietorships that continue to need assistance to access available resources such as business development counseling and small business loans. The AAPI community also continues to face barriers to employment and workplace advancement. Specific challenges experienced by AAPI subgroups include lower college-enrollment rates by Pacific Islanders than other ethnic groups and high poverty rates among Hmong Americans, Cambodian Americans, Malaysian Americans, and other individual AAPI communities. Additionally, one in five non-elderly AAPIs lacks health insurance.

The purpose of this order is to establish a President's Advisory Commission on Asian Americans and Pacific Islanders and a White House Initiative on Asian Americans and Pacific Islanders. Each will work to improve the quality of life and opportunities for Asian Americans and Pacific Islanders through increased access to, and participation in, Federal programs in which they may be underserved. In addition, each will work to advance relevant evidence-based research, data collection, and analysis for AAPI populations and subpopulations.

Sec. 2. President's Advisory Commission on Asian Americans and Pacific Islanders. There is established in the Department of Education the President's Advisory Commission on Asian Americans and Pacific Islanders (Commission).

   a. Mission and Function of the Commission. The Commission shall provide advice to the President, through the Secretaries of Education and Commerce, as Co-Chairs of the Initiative described in section 3 of this order, on: (i) the development, monitoring, and coordination of executive branch efforts to improve the quality of life of AAPIs through increased participation in Federal programs in which such persons may be underserved; (ii) the compilation of research and data related to AAPI populations and subpopulations; (iii) the development, monitoring, and coordination of Federal efforts to improve the economic and community development of AAPI businesses; and (iv) strategies to increase public and private-sector collaboration, and community involvement in improving the health, education, environment, and well-being of AAPIs.
   b. Membership of the Commission. The Commission shall consist of not more than 20 members appointed by the President. The Commission shall include members who: (i) have a history of involvement with the AAPI communities; (ii) are from the fields of education, commerce, business, health, human services, housing, environment, arts, agriculture, labor and employment, transportation, justice, veterans affairs, and economic and community development; (iii) are from civic associations representing one or more of the diverse AAPI communities; or (iv) have such other experience as the President deems appropriate. The President shall designate one member of the Commission to serve as Chair, who shall convene regular meetings of the Commission, determine its agenda, and direct its work.
   c. Administration of the Commission. The Secretary of Education, in consultation with the Secretary of Commerce, shall designate an Executive Director for the Commission. The Department of Education shall provide funding and administrative support for the Commission to the extent permitted by law and within

existing appropriations. Members of the Commission shall serve without compensation, but shall be allowed travel expenses, including per diem in lieu of subsistence, as authorized by law for persons serving intermittently in the Government service (5 U.S.C. 5701-5707). Insofar as the Federal Advisory Committee Act, as amended (5 U.S.C. App.) (the "Act"),may apply to the administration of the Commission, any functions of the President under the Act, except that of reporting to the Congress, shall be performed by the Secretary of Education, in accordance with the guidelines issued by the Administrator of General Services.

d. <u>Termination Date.</u> The Commission shall terminate 2 years from the date of this order, unless renewed by the President.

Sec. 3. White House Initiative on Asian Americans and Pacific Islanders. There is established the White House Initiative on Asian Americans and Pacific Islanders (Initiative), a Federal interagency working group whose members shall be selected by their respective agencies. The Secretary of Commerce and the Secretary of Education shall serve as the Co-Chairs of the Initiative. The Executive Director of the Commission established in section 2 of this order shall also serve as the Executive Director of the Initiative and shall report to the Secretaries on Initiative matters.

a. <u>Mission and Function of the Initiative.</u> The Initiative shall work to improve the quality of life of AAPIs through increased participation in Federal programs in which AAPIs may be underserved. The Initiative shall advise the Co-Chairs on the implementation and coordination of Federal programs as they relate to AAPIs across executive departments and agencies.
b. <u>Membership of the Initiative.</u> In addition to the Co-Chairs, the Initiative shall consist of senior officials from the following executive branch departments, agencies, and offices:
    i. the Department of State;
    ii. the Department of the Treasury;
    iii. the Department of Defense;
    iv. the Department of Justice;
    v. the Department of the Interior;
    vi. the Department of Agriculture;
    vii. the Department of Labor;
    viii. the Department of Housing and Urban Development;
    ix. the Department of Transportation;
    x. the Department of Energy;
    xi. the Department of Health and Human Services;
    xii. the Department of Veterans Affairs;
    xiii. the Department of Homeland Security;
    xiv. the Office of Management and Budget;
    xv. the Environmental Protection Agency;
    xvi. the Small Business Administration;
    xvii. the Office of Personnel Management;
    xviii. the Social Security Administration;
    xix. the White House Office of Cabinet Affairs;
    xx. the White House Office of Intergovernmental Affairs and Public Engagement;
    xxi. the National Economic Council;
    xxii. the Domestic Policy Council;
    xxiii. the Office of Science and Technology Policy; and
    xxiv. other executive branch departments, agencies, and offices as the President may, from time to time, designate.

    At the direction of the Co-Chairs, the Initiative may establish subgroups consisting exclusively of Initiative members or their designees under this section, as appropriate.
c. <u>Administration of the Initiative.</u> The Department of Education shall provide funding and administrative support for the Initiative to the extent permitted by law and within existing appropriations. The Co-Chairs shall convene regular meetings of the Initiative, determine its agenda, and direct its work.
d. <u>Federal Agency Plans and Interagency Plan.</u> Each executive department and agency designated by the Initiative shall prepare a plan (agency plan) for, and shall document, its efforts to improve the quality of

life of Asian Americans and Pacific Islanders through increased participation in Federal programs in which Asian Americans and Pacific Islanders may be underserved. Where appropriate, this agency plan shall address, among other things, the agency's efforts to:

  i.   identify Federal programs in which AAPIs may be underserved and improve the quality of life for AAPIs through increased participation in these programs;
  ii.   identify ways to foster the recruitment, career development, and advancement of AAPIs in the Federal Government;
  iii. identify high-priority action items for which measurable progress may be achieved within 2 years to improve the health, environment, opportunity, and well-being of AAPIs, and implement those action items;
  iv.   increase public-sector, private-sector, and community involvement in improving the health, environment, opportunity, and well-being of AAPIs;
  v.   foster evidence-based research, data-collection, and analysis on AAPI populations and subpopulations, including research and data on public health, environment, education, housing, employment, and other economic indicators of AAPI community wellbeing; and
  vi.   solicit public input from AAPI communities on ways to increase and improve opportunities for public participation in Federal programs considering a number of factors, including language barriers.

Each agency, in its plan, shall provide appropriate measurable objectives and, after the first year, shall provide for the assessment of that agency's performance on the goals set in the previous year's plan. Each agency plan shall be submitted to the Co-Chairs by a date to be established by the Co-Chairs. The Co-Chairs shall review the agency plans and develop for submission to the President a Federal interagency plan to improve the quality of life of AAPIs through increased participation in Federal programs in which such persons may be underserved. Actions described in the Federal interagency plan shall address improving access by AAPIs to Federal programs and fostering advances in relevant research and data.

Sec. 4. General Provisions.

  a.   This order supersedes Executive Order 13125 of June 7,1999, and Executive Order 13339 of May 13, 2004.
  b.   The heads of executive departments and agencies shall assist and provide information to the Commission, consistent with applicable law, as may be necessary to carry out the functions of the Commission. Each executive department and agency shall bear its own expenses of participating in the Commission.
  c.   Nothing in this order shall be construed to impair or otherwise affect:
      i.   authority granted by law to an executive department, agency, or the head thereof; or
      ii.   functions of the Director of the Office of Management and Budget relating to budgetary, administrative, or legislative proposals.
  d.   This order shall be implemented consistent with applicable law and subject to the availability of appropriations.
  e.   For purposes of this order, the term "Asian American and Pacific Islander" includes persons within the jurisdiction of the United States having ancestry of any of the original peoples of East Asia, Southeast Asia, or South Asia, or any of the aboriginal, indigenous, or native peoples of Hawaii and other Pacific Islands.
  f.   This order is not intended to, and does not, create any right or benefit, substantive or procedural, enforceable at law or in equity by any party against the United States, its departments, agencies, or entities, its officers, employees, or agents, or any other person.

Barack Obama
The White House,
October 14, 2009

APPENDIX B: Interagency Working Group Members

Co-chairs

U.S. Department of Commerce   Gary Locke, Secretary
U.S. Department of Education   Arne Duncan, Secretary

Executive Office of the President

National Economic Council	Ginger Lew, Senior Advisor and SBA Administrator
Office of Cabinet Affairs	Chris Lu, Assistant to the President and Cabinet Secretary
Office of the First Lady	Tina Tchen, Assistant to the President and Chief of Staff
Office of Intergovernmental Affairs	Nicholas Rathod, Associate Director
Office of Management and Budget	Preeta Bansal, General Counsel and Senior Policy Advisor
Office of Public Engagement	Bryan Jung, Director of Special Projects
Office of Science and Technology Policy	Kei Koizumi, Asst. Dir. for Fed. Research and Developmt.
Office of Social Innovation and Participation	Sonal Shah, Director

Federal Agencies

Corporation for National and Community Service	Patrick Corvington, CEO
Federal Communications Commission	--in transition--
National Aeronautics and Space Administration	Jaiwon Shin, Associate Administrator
U.S. Department of Agriculture	Kathleen Merrigan, Deputy Secretary
U.S. Department of Defense	Teri Takai, Chief Information Officer
U.S. Department of Energy	Bill Valdez, Director of Economic Impact and Diversity
U.S. Department of Health and Human Services	Dr. Howard Koh, Assistant Secretary
U.S. Department of Homeland Security	Ivan Fong, General Counsel
U.S. Department of Housing and Urban Development	Ron Sims, Deputy Secretary
U.S. Department of Interior	Anthony Babauta, Assistant Secretary
U.S. Department of Justice	Marisa Chun, Deputy Associate Attorney General
	Neal Katyal, Acting Solicitor General
U.S. Department of Labor	Patricia Shiu, Director of Federal Contract Compliance
U.S. Department of State	John Robinson, Chief Diversity Officer
U.S. Department of Transportation	David Kim, Deputy Assistant Secretary
U.S. Department of Treasury	Sharon Yuan, Deputy Assistant Secretary
U.S. Department of Veterans Affairs	Tammy Duckworth, Assistant Secretary
U.S. Environmental Protection Agency	Mathy Stanislaus, Assistant Administrator
U.S. Equal Employment Opportunity Commission	Stuart Ishimaru, Commissioner
U.S. Office of Personnel Management	Christine Griffin, Deputy Director
U.S. Small Business Administration	Ana Ma, Chief of Staff
U.S. Social Security Administration	Aviva Sufian, Associate Commissioner

Daphne Kwok, Chair
Executive Director of Asians and Pacific Islanders with Disabilities of California
San Francisco, CA

Sefa Aina, Vice Chair
Director of the Asian American Resource Center at Pomona College
Claremont, CA

Debra T. Cabrera
Faculty at St. John's School
Tumon, Guam

Kamuela J. N. Enos
Director of Community Resource Development at MA`O Organic Farms
Wai`anae, HI

Frances Eneski Francis
Partner at Spiegel & McDiarmid LLP
Washington, DC

Farooq Kathwari
Chairman, President and Chief Executive Officer of Ethan Allen Interiors
Danbury, CT

Hyeok Kim
Executive Director of InterIm Community Development Association
Seattle, WA

Ramey Ko
Associate Judge of the City of Austin Municipal Court
Austin, TX

Rozita Villanueva Lee
National Vice Chair of the National Federation of Filipino American Associations
Las Vegas, NV

Sunil Puri
President and Owner of First Rockford Group, Inc.
Chicago, IL

Amardeep Singh
Co-founder and Director of Programs at the Sikh Coalition
New York, NY

Unmi Song
Executive Director of the Lloyd A. Fry Foundation
Chicago, IL

Dilawar A. Syed
President and CEO of Yonja Media Group
San Francisco, CA

Dr. Khampha Thephavong
Primary Care Physician at the Veterans Affairs Hospital
Fresno, CA

Doua Thor
Executive Director of Southeast Asia Resource Action Center
Washington, DC

Hector L. Vargas, Jr.
Executive Director of the Gay & Lesbian Medical Association
Washington, DC

Hines Ward
Professional Football Player for the Pittsburgh Steelers
Pittsburgh, PA

www.ingramcontent.com/pod-product-compliance
Lightning Source LLC
Chambersburg PA
CBHW080756290526
45790CB00008B/3467